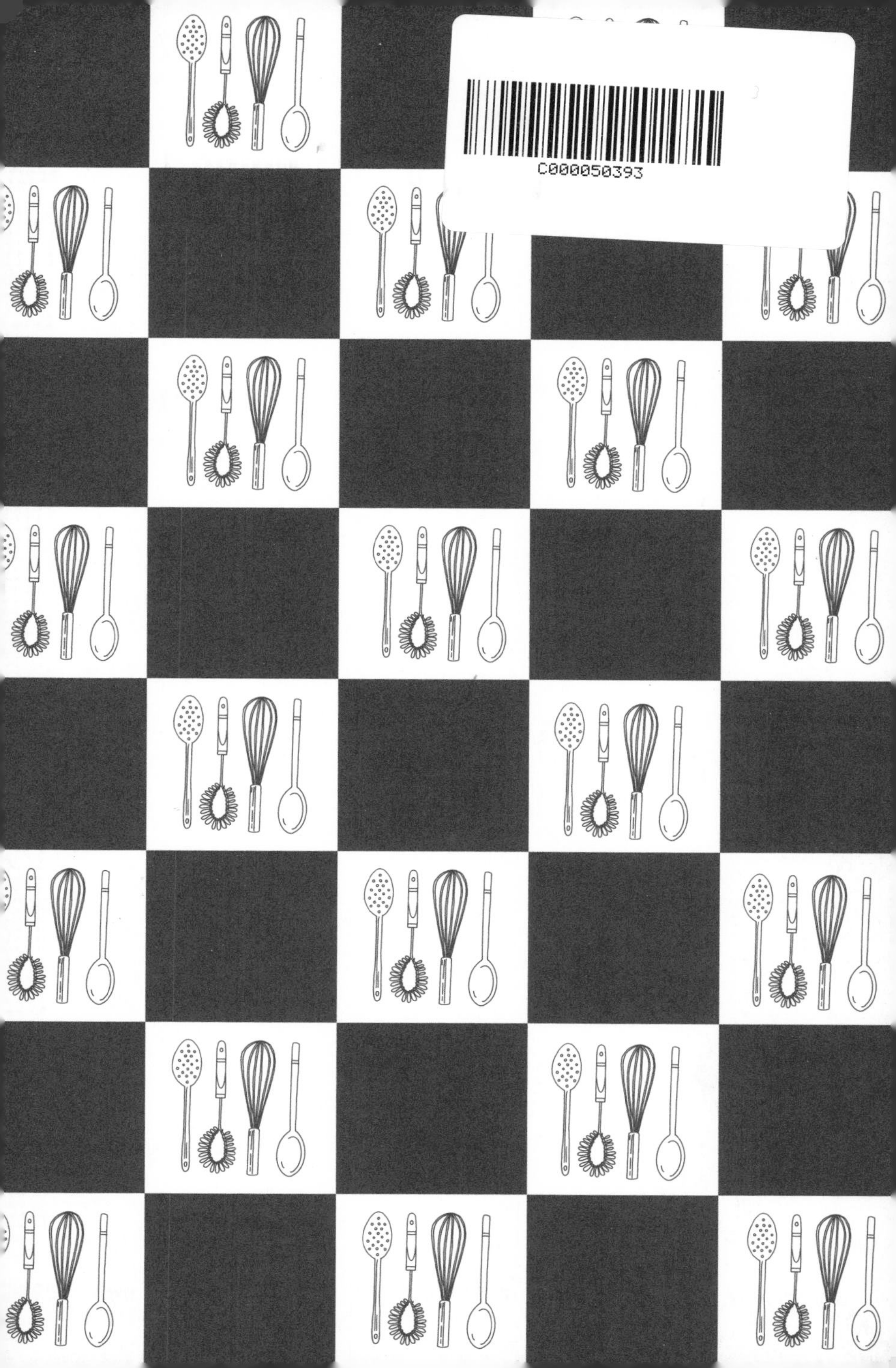

FOOD
PROCESSOR
COOKBOOK

Valerie Ferguson

LORENZ BOOKS

Contents

Introduction

How did we manage before the invention of the food processor? This amazing kitchen appliance really does take all the hard work out of food preparation – chopping, mincing, puréeing, grating, slicing, whisking and blending, making pastry, dough, batter and cake mixtures in a fraction of the usual time and with fabulous results.

Various attachments perform these functions. The most commonly used are the metal blade (for chopping vegetables, herbs, meat and fish; puréeing fruit, vegetables, soups and sauces; and making pastry and cakes); the slicing disc (for slicing vegetables); the grating disc (for grating cheese, chocolate, vegetables and fruit); and the dough hook or blade (for kneading bread dough). Food processors are available in a range of sizes, and many of the larger ones come with an additional small bowl for processing small quantities.

This book offers a selection of recipes to introduce you to the main functions of the processor, and each recipe clearly indicates which of the attachments to use. They will help you become accustomed to using your processor, show you its versatility and encourage you to get the best from this miracle machine.

Techniques

A food processor can be used for many different food preparation tasks.

Puréeing Vegetables
Fit the metal blade. Place the cooked vegetables in the bowl. Process until the vegetables have reached a smooth consistency, scraping down the sides of the bowl with a spatula as necessary.

Puréeing Greens
Before cooking, remove the tough stalks of leaves such as spinach. Drain thoroughly after cooking, gently squeezing the leaves to remove as much water as possible. Place the cooked leaves in the bowl of a food processor fitted with the metal blade and process until smooth.

Mincing (grinding) Meat
Using a sharp knife, trim the meat of all fat, gristle and bone and cut it into cubes. Place the meat in the bowl of a food processor fitted with the metal blade and pulse. Take care not to overprocess the meat: stop the machine every 5–10 seconds and stir to ensure even mincing.

Pulping Fresh Ginger
Peel the ginger and cut into fairly small pieces. Place the ginger in the bowl of a food processor fitted with the metal blade and process, adding a little water if necessary until the ginger has reached the right consistency. Store in an airtight container in the refrigerator for 4–6 weeks or freeze in ice-cube trays kept for the purpose.

Pulping Garlic
Remove the skin from the garlic and place the whole cloves in the bowl of a food processor fitted with the metal blade. Process until smooth. Store as for pulped ginger.

Making Pizza Dough

Fit the dough blade or hook and process the dry ingredients to mix. With the machine running, pour the liquid through the feed tube and process until the dough forms a soft ball. Rest for 2 minutes, then process for 1 minute to knead. Leave the dough in a warm place for 1 hour to rise, then knock back and knead again before use.

Grating Chocolate

Use the grater attachment and pusher to feed the chocolate through the processor. For very fine shavings you can use the metal blade, but first be sure that the chocolate is soft enough to pierce with a sharp knife. Cut it into small pieces and, with the machine running, drop these through the feed tube.

Grinding Nuts

It is not easy to achieve an even texture when grinding nuts in a food processor and thus there is a risk of overworking them to a paste. To prevent this, try grinding the nuts with some of the sugar or flour called for in the recipe.

Making a Fruit Sauce

Stone and peel the fruit, if necessary, and cut large fruit into pieces. Place with lemon juice and sugar in a food processor fitted with the metal blade. Process until a purée is formed, scraping down the sides of the bowl once. Stir in a little brandy or another liqueur, if you wish. Sieve soft fruit purées. Chill the sauce before use.

Tips for Success

• Familiarize yourself with your food processor and all its accessories before you start to cook.
• The blades are very sharp, so treat them with respect, and take great care when cleaning.
• Keep your machine in a central position in the kitchen.
• Always allow food to cool slightly before processing.
• Never remove the lid before switching off the machine.
• Never be tempted to push food down the feed tube with your hand, but use the pusher supplied.
• Always check the maximum volume your machine can cope with: overloading can cause damage.

Simple Sauces

Mayonnaise

With a food processor, home-made mayonnaise could not be easier.

Makes about 350 ml/
12 fl oz/1½ cups

INGREDIENTS
2 egg yolks
15 ml/1 tbsp Dijon mustard
15 ml/1 tbsp white wine vinegar
300 ml/½ pint/1¼ cups olive oil or half olive
    oil and half sunflower oil
15–30 ml/1–2 tbsp boiling water

Metal blade

1 Put the egg yolks in the bowl of a food processor, fitted with the metal blade. Add the mustard and vinegar and process for 10 seconds to blend.

2 With the machine running, gradually pour in the oil through the feeder tube in a steady stream until all the oil is incorporated and the sauce is thickened. Add the boiling water and process briefly. Store the mayonnaise in the refrigerator for up to 2–3 days.

Easy Pesto Sauce

Take all the hard work out of making pesto by using a food processor.

Makes about 300 ml/
½ pint/1¼ cups

INGREDIENTS
50 g/2 oz/about 2 cups fresh
    basil leaves
1–2 garlic cloves
45 ml/3 tbsp grated Parmesan cheese
45 ml/3 tbsp pine nuts, lightly toasted
60–90 ml/4–6 tbsp virgin olive oil, plus
    extra for sealing
salt and freshly ground
    black pepper

Metal blade

1 Put the fresh basil leaves, garlic, grated Parmesan cheese and toasted pine nuts in the bowl of a food processor, fitted with the metal blade. Season with salt and freshly ground black pepper and process until well blended, scraping down the side of the bowl once or twice.

2 With the machine running, gradually pour the oil through the feed tube until a smooth paste forms. Pour into a jar and spoon over a little more oil to seal the surface.

3 Cover tightly and store in the refrigerator for up to 1 week, or freeze in smaller quantities.

Special Tomato Sauce

Your food processor will prove a boon
for making this versatile sauce.

Makes about 450 ml/
¾ pint/scant 2 cups

INGREDIENTS
675 g/1½ lb tomatoes, fresh or canned,
    chopped in a food processor
1 carrot, chopped in a food processor
1 celery stick, chopped in a food processor
1 medium onion, chopped in a
    food processor
1 garlic clove, crushed
75 ml/5 tbsp olive oil
a few fresh basil leaves or a small pinch of
    dried oregano
salt and freshly ground black pepper

Metal blade

1 Place all the ingredients in a
heavy-based pan and simmer for 30
minutes. Purée the sauce in a food
processor, fitted with the metal blade.

2 Return to the pan, adjust the
seasoning and simmer for 15 minutes.
It can be stored in the refrigerator for
up to 4 days.

Barbecue Sauce

Brush this sauce over meat before
barbecuing, or serve it alongside.

Makes about 300 ml/
½ pint/1¼ cups

INGREDIENTS
30 ml/2 tbsp vegetable oil
1 large onion, chopped in a food processor
2 garlic cloves, crushed
400 g/14 oz can tomatoes
30 ml/2 tbsp Worcestershire sauce
15 ml/1 tbsp white wine vinegar
45 ml/3 tbsp honey
5 ml/1 tsp mustard powder
2.5 ml/½ tsp mild chilli powder
salt and freshly ground black pepper

Metal blade

1 Heat the oil and fry the onions and
garlic until soft. Stir in the remaining
ingredients and simmer, uncovered, for
15–20 minutes, stirring occasionally.
Cool slightly.

2 Pour into the bowl of a food
processor, fitted with the metal blade.
Process until smooth. Store in the
refrigerator for up to 4 days.

Gazpacho

For this traditional, chilled Spanish soup, which requires all the ingredients to be finely chopped or puréed, a food processor really does save time.

Serves 6

INGREDIENTS
1 green (bell) pepper, seeded and chopped
1 red (bell) pepper, seeded and chopped
½ cucumber, roughly chopped
1 onion, roughly chopped
1 fresh red chilli, seeded and
   roughly chopped
450 g/1 lb ripe plum tomatoes,
   roughly chopped
900 ml/1½ pints/3¾ cups passata or
   tomato juice
30 ml/2 tbsp red wine vinegar
30 ml/2 tbsp olive oil
15 ml/1 tbsp caster (superfine) sugar
salt and freshly ground black pepper
crushed ice, to garnish (optional)

Metal blade

1 Reserve a small piece each of green and red pepper, cucumber and onion. Using a small, sharp knife chop finely. Set aside, covered with clear film, for the garnish.

2 Process all the remaining ingredients (except the ice) in the food processor until smooth. You may need to do this in batches.

3 Pass the soup through a sieve into a clean glass bowl, pushing it through with a spoon to extract as much flavour as possible.

4 Adjust the seasoning to taste and chill. Serve sprinkled with the reserved finely chopped peppers, cucumber and onion. For an extra-special touch, add a little crushed ice to the garnish.

Cream of Courgette Soup

Use your food processor both for slicing the raw courgettes (zucchini) and for puréeing this subtle-tasting soup after cooking.

Serves 4–6

INGREDIENTS
30 ml/2 tbsp olive oil
15 g/½ oz/1 tbsp butter
1 onion, chopped in a food processor
900 g/2 lb courgettes (zucchini), trimmed
    and sliced in a food processor
5 ml/1 tsp dried oregano
about 600 ml/1 pint/2½ cups vegetable
    or chicken stock
115 g/4 oz dolcelatte cheese, rind
    removed, diced
300 ml/½ pint/1¼ cups single (light) cream
salt and freshly ground black pepper
fresh oregano, extra diced dolcelatte and
    ground black pepper, to garnish

Slicing disc
Metal blade

2 Add the courgettes and oregano, with salt and pepper to taste. Cook over a medium heat for 10 minutes, stirring frequently.

3 Pour in most of the stock and bring to the boil, stirring. Lower the heat, half cover the pan and allow to simmer gently, stirring occasionally, for about 30 minutes. Stir in the dolcelatte until melted. Allow to cool slightly.

1 Heat the oil and butter in a large pan until foaming. Add the onion and cook gently for about 5 minutes, stirring frequently, until softened but not brown.

4 Process the soup until smooth in a food processor, fitted with the metal blade, then press through a sieve into a clean pan. Scrape the underside of the sieve to obtain all the purée.

5 Add two-thirds of the cream and stir over a low heat until hot, but not boiling. Check the consistency and add more vegetable or chicken stock if the soup is too thick.

6 Adjust the seasoning to taste, then pour into warmed bowls. Swirl in the remaining cream. Garnish with fresh oregano, extra diced cheese and ground pepper and serve immediately.

Jerusalem Artichoke Soup

A distinctive, creamy soup, easily made using a food processor.

Serves 4

INGREDIENTS
25–50 g/1–2 oz/2–4 tbsp butter
115 g/4 oz/generous 1½ cups sliced
    mushrooms, prepared in a food processor
2 onions, chopped in a food processor
450 g/1 lb Jerusalem artichokes, peeled and
    sliced in a food processor
300 ml/½ pint/1¼ cups vegetable stock
300 ml/½ pint/1¼ cups milk
salt and freshly ground black pepper

Slicing disc
Metal blade

1 Melt the butter in a pan and sauté the mushrooms for 1 minute. Set aside. Sauté the onions and artichokes, adding a little more butter to the pan if needed. Keep on stirring the vegetables without allowing them to brown.

2 Add the stock and bring to the boil. Simmer for 15 minutes, until the artichokes are soft and then season.

3 Purée in a food processor, fitted with the metal blade, adding the milk through the feed tube until smooth. Reheat with the mushrooms and serve.

Tomato & Red Pepper Soup

With a food processor, this late summer soup is even easier.

Serves 4

INGREDIENTS
30–60 ml/2–4 tbsp olive oil
1 onion, chopped in a food processor
450 g/1 lb red or orange (bell) peppers,
    thinly sliced in a food processor
5 large tomatoes, peeled and chopped in a
    food processor
30 ml/2 tbsp tomato purée (paste)
pinch of sugar
475 ml/16 fl oz/2 cups vegetable stock
salt and freshly ground black pepper
chopped fresh dill, to garnish

Metal blade

1 Heat half the oil in a pan and sauté the onion until soft. Add the peppers and the remaining oil. Cook, without browning until starting to soften.

2 Add the tomatoes, purée, seasoning, sugar and a little stock. Simmer for 10 minutes or until tender. Add the remaining stock. Purée in a food processor, fitted with the metal blade, then sieve, garnish and serve.

Right: Jerusalem Artichoke Soup (top); Tomato & Red Pepper Soup

Chicken Kebabs with Satay Sauce

A wonderful spicy marinade for the chicken is made in moments in a food processor, as is the delicious peanut sauce to serve alongside.

Makes about 24

INGREDIENTS
450 g/1 lb boneless, skinless chicken breasts
oil, for brushing
fresh coriander (cilantro) and coconut
    shavings, to garnish

FOR THE MARINADE
90 ml/6 tbsp vegetable oil
60 ml/4 tbsp tamari or light soy sauce
60 ml/4 tbsp lime juice
2.5 cm/½ in piece fresh root ginger, peeled
    and chopped
3–4 garlic cloves
30 ml/2 tbsp light brown sugar
5 ml/1 tsp Chinese-style chilli sauce or
    1 small fresh red chilli pepper, seeded
    and chopped
30 ml/2 tbsp chopped fresh coriander
    (cilantro)

FOR THE PEANUT SAUCE
30 ml/2 tbsp smooth peanut butter
30 ml/2 tbsp soy sauce
15 ml/1 tbsp sesame or vegetable oil
2 spring onions (scallions), chopped
2 garlic cloves
15–30 ml/1–2 tbsp lime or
    lemon juice
15 ml/1 tbsp brown sugar

Metal blade

1 To make the marinade, place all the marinade ingredients in the bowl of a food processor, fitted with the metal blade. Process until smooth, scraping down the sides of the bowl once. Pour into a shallow dish and set aside.

2 To make the peanut sauce, place all the peanut sauce ingredients into the food processor and process until well blended. If the sauce is too thick, add a little water and process again. Pour into a bowl and cover until needed.

3 Put the chicken breasts in the freezer for 5 minutes to firm. Slice the chicken breasts in half horizontally, then into thin strips. Cut the strips into 2 cm/¾ in pieces.

4 Add the chicken to the marinade in the dish. Toss well, then cover and marinate for 3–4 hours in a cool place, or overnight in the refrigerator.

5 Preheat the grill (broiler). Line a baking sheet with foil and brush lightly with oil. Thread two or three pieces of marinated chicken on to skewers and grill (broil) for 4–5 minutes, turning once. Serve with the peanut sauce and a garnish of fresh coriander and coconut shavings.

COOK'S TIP: When using metal skewers, look for flat ones which prevent the food from spinning around. If using wooden skewers, be sure to soak them in cold water for at least 30 minutes, to prevent them from burning.

Sesame Prawn Toasts

A food processor makes light work of the prawn paste for these toasts.

Serves 6

INGREDIENTS

175 g/6 oz peeled prawns (shrimp)
2 spring onions (scallions), chopped
2.5 cm/1 in piece root ginger, peeled and
    roughly chopped
2 garlic cloves, crushed
25 g/1 oz/2 tbsp cornflour (cornstarch)
10 ml/2 tsp soy sauce, plus extra
    for dipping
6 slices stale bread from a small loaf,
    crusts removed
40 g/1½ oz/3 tbsp sesame seeds
about 600 ml/1 pint/2½ cups vegetable oil,
    for deep-frying

Metal blade

1 Place the prawns, spring onions, ginger and garlic in a food processor, fitted with the metal blade. Add the cornflour and soy sauce and process to a thick paste.

2 Spread the bread slices evenly with the paste and cut into triangles. Sprinkle with the sesame seeds and make sure they stick to the paste. Chill for 30 minutes.

3 Heat the oil in a heavy-based pan until it reaches 190°C/375°F. Using a slotted spoon, lower the toasts in batches into the oil, sesame-side down, and fry for 2–3 minutes, turning for the last minute. Drain on kitchen paper. Serve with soy sauce.

Asparagus with Hollandaise

This tasty Hollandaise sauce is flavoured with tarragon.

Serves 4

INGREDIENTS
500 g/1¼ lb fresh asparagus, prepared
salt

FOR THE HOLLANDAISE SAUCE
2 egg yolks
15 ml/1 tbsp lemon juice
115 g/4 oz/½ cup butter
10 ml/2 tsp finely chopped fresh tarragon
salt and freshly ground black pepper

Metal blade

1 Lay the asparagus in a steamer, add water, then cover and steam for 6–10 minutes until tender depending on the thickness of the stems.

2 To make the Hollandaise sauce, place the egg yolks, lemon juice and seasoning in the bowl of a food processor, fitted with the metal blade, and process briefly.

3 Melt the butter in a small pan until foaming and then, with the machine running, pour it on to the egg mixture in a slow, steady stream.

4 Stir in the tarragon by hand for a sauce speckled with green, or process it for a pale green sauce.

5 Arrange the asparagus on plates and pour over some of the Hollandaise sauce. Sprinkle with pepper. Serve the remaining sauce in a jug.

Spiced Carrot Dip

Sweet-and-spicy carrots are transformed with the aid of a food processor.

Serves 4

INGREDIENTS
3 carrots, plus extra to garnish
1 onion
grated rind (zest) and juice of 2 oranges
15 ml/1 tbsp hot curry paste
150 ml/¼ pint/⅔ cup plain (all-purpose)
    yogurt
handful of fresh basil leaves
15–30 ml/1–2 tbsp lemon juice, to taste
Tabasco sauce, to taste
salt and freshly ground black pepper

Grating disc, Metal blade

1 Grate the carrots in a food
processor, fitted with a grating disc;
reserve a little for the garnish. Fit the
metal blade and finely chop the onion.

2 Place the onion, carrots, orange rind
and juice and curry paste in a small
saucepan. Bring to the boil, cover and
simmer for 10 minutes until tender.

3 Process in the food processor until
smooth. Leave to cool, then stir in the
yogurt. Tear the basil into small pieces
and stir into the mixture.

4 Add the lemon juice, Tabasco and
salt and pepper to taste. Serve within
a few hours at room temperature,
garnished with the reserved carrot.

VARIATION: Greek-style yogurt
or soured cream may be used in
place of the yogurt to make a
richer, creamy dip.

Saucy Tomato Dip

What could be easier than this refreshing dip, whizzed up in your processor?

Serves 4

INGREDIENTS
1 shallot
2 garlic cloves
handful of fresh basil leaves, plus extra
    to garnish
500 g/1¼ lb ripe tomatoes
30 ml/2 tbsp olive oil
2 fresh green chillies
salt and fresh ground black pepper

Metal blade

1 Peel and halve the shallot and garlic cloves. Place in a food processor, fitted with the metal blade, and add the basil leaves. Process until very finely chopped.

2 Halve the tomatoes and add to the shallot mixture. Pulse until the mixture is well blended and the tomatoes are finely chopped. With the machine running, slowly pour in the olive oil through the feed tube. Season to taste.

3 Halve the chillies lengthways and remove the seeds. Finely slice them across into tiny strips and stir into the tomato mixture. Serve at room temperature, garnished with a few torn basil leaves, coarse sea salt and pepper.

COOK'S TIP: This dip is best made with full-flavoured sun-ripened tomatoes. In winter, use a drained 400 g/10 oz can of plum tomatoes.

Aubergine & Pepper Spread

Here a food processor is invaluable.

Serves 6–8

INGREDIENTS
675 g/1½ lb aubergines (eggplant), halved
     lengthways
2 green (bell) peppers, seeded and quartered
45 ml/3 tbsp olive oil
2 firm ripe tomatoes, halved, seeded and
     finely chopped in a food processor
45 ml/3 tbsp chopped fresh parsley
     or coriander (cilantro), plus a few whole
     sprigs to garnish
2 garlic cloves, crushed
30 ml/2 tbsp red wine vinegar
lemon juice, to taste
salt and freshly ground black pepper
dark rye bread and lemon wedges, to serve

Metal blade

1 Preheat the grill (broiler). Grill
(broil) the aubergines and peppers,
skin-side uppermost, until blistered.
Turn over and cook for a further 3
minutes. Place in a polythene bag for
10 minutes. Peel away the skin and
purée the flesh in a food processor.
With the machine running, pour olive
oil steadily through the feed tube.

2 Remove the blade, stir in the
remaining ingredients and transfer to a
bowl. Garnish with herbs sprigs and
serve with bread and lemon wedges.

Taramasalata

Purée the cod's roe for this
delicious Mediterranean classic
in a food processor.

Serves 4–6

INGREDIENTS
115 g/4 oz/8 tbsp smoked cod's roe
15 ml/1 tbsp lemon juice
175 ml/6 fl oz/¾ cup olive oil, plus a little
     extra for drizzling
20 g/¾ oz finely grated onion
15–25 ml/1–1½ tbsp boiling water
paprika, for sprinkling
black olives and celery leaves, to garnish

Metal blade

1 Soak the cod's roe in cold water
for 2 hours. Drain, then peel off and
discard any outer skin and membrane.
Process the roe at low speed in a food
processor, fitted with the metal blade.

2 Add the lemon juice and then,
with the machine still running, slowly
add the oil through the feed tube.

3 When the mixture has thickened,
beat in the onion and water. Spoon
into a serving bowl and chill well.
Sprinkle with a little paprika. Garnish
with the olives and celery leaves and
drizzle with a little oil. This is very
good served with toasted bread.

*Right: Aubergine & Pepper Spread (top);
Taramasalata*

Smoked Salmon Pâté

This luxurious pâté takes scarcely any time to prepare with a food processor and looks most impressive.

Serves 4

INGREDIENTS
350 g/12 oz thinly sliced smoked salmon
150 ml/¼ pint/⅔ cup double (heavy) cream
finely grated rind (zest) and juice of 1 lemon
salt and freshly ground black pepper
fresh dill, to garnish
melba toast, to serve

Metal blade

1 Line four small ramekin dishes with clear film, then line with 115 g/4 oz of the smoked salmon cut into strips long enough to flop over the edges.

2 In a food processor, fitted with the metal blade, process the remaining salmon with the seasoning, double cream and lemon rind and juice.

3 Pack the lined ramekins with the smoked salmon pâté and wrap over the loose strips of salmon. Cover and chill for 30 minutes, then turn out of the moulds, garnish with dill and serve with melba toast.

COOK'S TIP: Process the salmon in short bursts until it is just smooth. Don't overprocess the pâté or it will thicken too much.

Chicken Liver Pâté

Use your food processor to make this rich-tasting, smooth pâté, and you will be sure to achieve perfect results.

Serves 4

INGREDIENTS
115 g/4 oz chicken livers, thawed if
    frozen, trimmed
1 small garlic clove, chopped
15 ml/1 tbsp sherry
30 ml/2 tbsp brandy
50 g/2 oz/¼ cup butter, melted
1.5 ml/¼ tsp salt
fresh herbs and black peppercorns, to garnish
warm bread, to serve

Metal blade

1 Preheat the oven to 150°C/300°F/ Gas 2. Place the chicken livers and garlic in a food processor, fitted with the metal blade. Process until smooth.

2 With the motor running, gradually add the sherry, brandy, melted butter and salt to the liver and garlic mixture through the feed tube.

3 Pour the mixture into two 7.5 cm/3 in ramekins and cover with foil. Place them in a roasting tin and slowly pour boiling water into the tin until it comes halfway up the sides of the dishes.

4 Carefully transfer the tin to the oven and bake for 20 minutes. Allow to cool to room temperature then remove the ramekins from the tin and chill until you are ready to serve. Garnish with herbs and black peppercorns and serve with warm bread.

Mushroom Picker's Pâté

A good vegetable pâté should be as smooth as one made with fine liver.
A food processor is useful for preparing and puréeing the vegetables.

Serves 4

INGREDIENTS
45 ml/3 tbsp vegetable oil
1 medium onion, chopped in a
    food processor
½ celery stick, chopped in a food processor
350 g/12 oz/5 cups assorted trimmed and
    sliced wild and cultivated mushrooms such
    as closed field (portobello) mushrooms,
    oyster and shiitake mushrooms,
    bay boletus and horn of plenty, sliced
    in a food processor
150 g/5 oz/⅔ cup red lentils
550 ml/18 fl oz/2½ cups vegetable stock
    or water
1 sprig fresh thyme
50 g/2 oz/¼ cup almond or cashew nut butter
1 garlic clove, crushed
25 g/1 oz bread, crusts removed
75 ml/5 tbsp milk
15 ml/1 tbsp lemon juice
4 egg yolks
celery salt and freshly ground black pepper
salad and toasted bread, to serve

Metal blade
Slicing disc

1 Preheat the oven to 180°C/350°F/
Gas 4. Heat the oil in a large pan, add
the onion and celery and brown
lightly. Add the mushrooms and soften
for 4 minutes. Remove a tablespoonful
of the mushrooms and set aside.

2 Add the lentils, stock or water and
thyme, bring to the boil, uncovered,
and simmer for 20 minutes or until
the lentils have fallen apart.

3 Place the nut butter, garlic, bread
and milk in a food processor, fitted
with the metal blade, and blend until
the mixture is smooth.

4 Add the lemon juice and egg yolks
and combine. Add the lentil mixture,
blend, then season well. Lastly stir the
reserved mushrooms into the mixture.

5 Turn the mixture into a 1.2 litre/ 2 pint/5 cup pâté dish, stand the dish in a roasting tin (pan) half filled with boiling water, cover and cook in the oven for 50 minutes.

6 Allow the mushroom pâté to cool before spooning from the dish and serving at room temperature, accompanied by mixed salad and toasted bread.

COOK'S TIPS: If you are using only cultivated mushrooms, an addition of 10 g/¼ oz dried ceps, bay boletus, chanterelles and horn of plenty will provide a good wild-mushroom flavour. Soak first in warm water for 20 minutes.

Almond or cashew nut butter is available from most good health-food shops.

Chicken & Pork Terrine

The ingredients for this delicately flavoured dish are processed together in a matter of seconds.

Serves 6–8

INGREDIENTS
225 g/8 oz rindless, streaky bacon
375 g/13 oz boneless, skinless
   chicken breasts
15 ml/1 tbsp lemon juice
225 g/8 oz minced (ground) pork
½ small onion, finely chopped in a
   food processor
2 eggs, beaten
30 ml/2 tbsp chopped fresh parsley
5 ml/1 tsp salt
5 ml/1 tsp green peppercorns, crushed
green salad, radishes and lemon wedges
   to serve

Metal blade

1 Preheat the oven to 160°C/325°F/ Gas 3. Put the bacon on a board and stretch it with the back of a knife so that it can be arranged in overlapping slices over the base and sides of a 900 g/2 lb loaf tin.

2 Cut 115 g/4 oz of the chicken into strips about 10 cm/4 in long. Sprinkle with lemon juice. Put the rest of the chicken in a food processor, fitted with the metal blade, and add the minced pork and the chopped onion. Process until fairly smooth.

3 Add the eggs, parsley, salt and peppercorns to the meat mixture and process again briefly. Spoon half the mixture into the loaf tin (pan) and then level the surface.

4 Arrange the chicken strips over this, then spoon in the remaining meat mixture and smooth the top. Give the tin a couple of taps to knock out any pockets of air. Trim the bacon edges.

5 Cover with a piece of oiled foil and put in a roasting tin. Pour in enough hot water to come halfway up the sides of the loaf tin. Bake for 45–50 minutes, or until firm.

6 Allow the terrine to cool in the tin before turning out and chilling. Serve sliced, with a green salad, radishes and wedges of lemon to squeeze over.

VARIATION: This terrine would also work well made with turkey breasts in place of the chicken.

Cod with Coriander Pesto Salsa

This aromatic salsa, made entirely in a food processor, is the perfect complement to grilled white fish such as cod.

Serves 4

INGREDIENTS
4 cod steaks, about 175 g/6 oz each
melted butter, for brushing
lime wedges, to serve

FOR THE PESTO SALSA
50 g/2 oz fresh coriander (cilantro) leaves
15 g/½ oz fresh parsley
2 fresh red chillies
1 garlic clove
50 g/2 oz/½ cup shelled pistachio nuts
25 g/1 oz/⅓ cup fresh Parmesan cheese, finely grated
90 ml/6 tbsp olive oil
juice of 2 limes
salt and freshly ground black pepper

Metal blade

1 To make the pesto salsa, chop the fresh coriander and parsley in a food processor, fitted with the metal blade.

VARIATIONS: Any number of different herbs or nuts may be used to make a similar salsa to this one – try a mixture of rosemary, parsley and walnuts. A handful of pitted black olives is another tasty addition.

2 Halve the chillies lengthways and remove their seeds. Add to the herbs, together with the garlic and process until finely chopped.

3 Add the pistachio nuts to the herb mixture and pulse the power until they are roughly chopped. Stir in the grated Parmesan cheese, olive oil and lime juice.

4 Add salt and pepper to taste. Spoon the mixture into a serving bowl, cover and chill until ready to serve.

5 Preheat the grill (broiler). Brush the cod steaks with melted butter and season. Grill (broil) for 5–6 minutes each side until cooked. Serve with lime wedges, accompanied by the salsa.

Herby Plaice Croquettes

Preparing the mixture for these fish croquettes – and the breadcrumbs for their coating – is so easy with a food processor.

Serves 4

INGREDIENTS
450 g/1 lb plaice fillets
300 ml/½ pint/1¼ cups milk
450 g/1 lb peeled, cooked potatoes
1 fennel bulb, finely chopped in a
    food processor
1 garlic clove, finely chopped in a
    food processor
45 ml/3 tbsp chopped fresh parsley
2 eggs
15 ml/1 tbsp unsalted butter
plain (all-purpose) flour, for dusting hands
225 g/8 oz/4 cups white breadcrumbs,
    made in a food processor
25 g/1 oz/2 tbsp sesame seeds
oil, for deep-frying
salt and freshly ground black pepper

Metal blade

2 Peel the skin off the fish and remove any bones. In a food processor, fitted with the metal blade, process the fish, potatoes, fennel, garlic, parsley, eggs and butter.

3 Add 30 ml/2 tbsp of the reserved cooking milk and season to taste. Chill for 30 minutes, then shape the mixture into 20 croquettes with floured hands.

4 Mix together the breadcrumbs and sesame seeds. Roll the croquettes in the mixture to form a good coating.

1 Poach the fish fillets in the milk for approximately 15 minutes until the fish flakes. Drain the fillets and reserve the milk.

5 Heat the oil in a large, heavy-based saucepan. Deep-fry the croquettes in batches for about 4 minutes until golden brown. Drain well on kitchen paper and serve hot.

VARIATION: If plaice fillets are unavailable, other white fish, such as sole, haddock or cod, could be used for these croquettes.

Cumin and Coriander Spiced Poussins

This cumin and coriander paste, quickly whizzed up in a food processor, gives the poussins a fabulous flavour and keeps them moist during the cooking process.

Serves 4

INGREDIENTS
2 garlic cloves
½ small onion
5 ml/1 tsp ground cumin
5 ml/1 tsp ground coriander
pinch of cayenne pepper
60 ml/4 tbsp olive oil
2.5 ml/½ tsp salt
2 poussins
lemon wedges, to garnish

Metal blade

1 Roughly chop the garlic and onion and place in the bowl of a food processor, fitted with the metal blade.

2 Add the cumin, coriander, cayenne pepper, olive oil and salt. Process to make a paste that will spread easily.

3 Cut the poussins in half lengthways. Place them skin-side up in a shallow, non-metallic dish and spread with the spice paste, making sure that they are evenly coated. Cover and leave them to marinate for at least 2 hours in the refrigerator.

4 Preheat the grill to medium. Grill the poussins on a rack for 15–20 minutes, turning frequently, until they are cooked through and lightly charred on the outside.

5 Place each half poussin on a warmed plate and serve immediately, garnished with lemon wedges.

VARIATION: Chicken portions and quail are also very good cooked in this way. You will need to adjust the cooking time accordingly.

Steak with Tapenade

Succulent marinated beef is roasted in a sensational coating of black olives and anchovies prepared in a food processor.

Serves 4

INGREDIENTS
large bunch of fresh rosemary
1.3 kg/3 lb trimmed fillet of beef, halved
4 garlic cloves, crushed
300 ml/½ pint/1¼ cups olive oil
salt and freshly ground black pepper
tomato salad, to serve

FOR THE TAPENADE
50 g/2 oz canned anchovies
115 g/4 oz/1 cup pitted black olives
2 garlic cloves
2 egg yolks
150 ml/¼ pint/⅔ cup olive oil
10 ml/2 tsp lemon juice

Metal blade

1 Reserving a few sprigs of rosemary for the garnish, in a shallow, non-metallic dish cover the beef with the rosemary, crushed garlic, oil and seasoning. Leave to marinate for at least 2 hours in the refrigerator.

2 To make the tapenade, drain the anchovies well and place them in a bowl of cold water to soak for about 20 minutes.

3 In a food processor, fitted with the metal blade, roughly chop the anchovies, olives and garlic cloves.

4 Add the egg yolks and gradually pour in the oil through the feed tube while the machine is still running. Add the lemon juice and season to taste. Chill for 30 minutes.

5 Preheat the oven to 190°C/375°F/ Gas 5. Spread the tapenade over the beef and cook in the oven for 45 minutes. Serve sliced, garnished with rosemary and accompanied by a tomato salad.

Beef & Mushroom Burgers

Really tasty burgers made without effort in your food processor.

Serves 4

INGREDIENTS
50 g/2 oz day-old bread, without crusts
1 small onion
150 g/5 oz/2 cups small cup mushrooms
450 g/1 lb minced (ground) beef
5 ml/1 tsp dried mixed herbs
15 ml/1 tbsp tomato purée (paste)
flour, for shaping
salt and freshly ground black pepper
burger buns, salad and relish, to garnish

Metal blade

1 Tear the bread into pieces and place in a food processor, fitted with the metal blade. Process briefly to form crumbs. Set aside.

2 Place the onion and mushrooms in the food processor and process until finely chopped. Add the beef, breadcrumbs, herbs, tomato purée and seasoning. Process for a few seconds until the mixture binds together but still has some texture.

3 Divide the mixture into eight to ten portions, then press into burger shapes using lightly floured hands.

4 Cook the burgers in a non-stick frying pan, or under a hot grill (broiler), for 12–15 minutes, turning once with a fish slice, until evenly cooked. Serve in buns, with salad and relish.

Meat Loaf

A food processor does all the chopping, crumbing and mincing required.

Serves 6

INGREDIENTS

225 g/8 oz/3 cups mushrooms, coarsely
    chopped in a food processor
1 small onion, chopped in a food processor
25 g/1 oz/2 tbsp butter
130 g/4½ oz breadcrumbs, made in a
    food processor
45 ml/3 tbsp chopped fresh parsley
5 ml/1 tsp dried thyme
10 ml/2 tsp bottled brown sauce
675 g/1½ lb lean beef, minced (ground) in a
    food processor
225 g/8 oz lean pork, minced (ground) in a
    food processor
75 ml/5 tbsp tomato ketchup
2 eggs, beaten
salt and freshly ground
    black pepper

Metal blade

1 Preheat the oven to 190°C/375°F/
Gas 5. Cook the mushrooms and onion
in the butter over moderate heat until
soft. Turn the mixture into a bowl. Add
the breadcrumbs, parsley, thyme, brown
sauce, salt and pepper. Mix well.

2 Place the beef, pork, ketchup, eggs
and seasoning in another bowl and
mix until thoroughly blended.

3 Pack half of the meat mixture into
a large loaf tin, pressing it into an even
layer. Pack the mushroom mixture on
top, then cover with the rest of the
meat. Bake for 1¼ hours.

4 Remove from the oven and leave
to stand for 15 minutes. Pour off the
juices, then turn out on to a serving
plate. Lightly cooked vegetables make
a good accompaniment.

Sesame Seed-coated Falafel with Tahini Yogurt Dip

Mix both the spicy chickpea paste for the falafel and the ingredients for the smooth dip in a food processor.

Serves 4

INGREDIENTS
250 g/9 oz/1⅓ cups dried chickpeas
2 garlic cloves, crushed
1 fresh red chilli, seeded and finely sliced
5 ml/1 tsp ground coriander
5 ml/1 tsp ground cumin
15 ml/1 tbsp chopped fresh mint
15 ml/1 tbsp chopped fresh parsley
2 spring onions (scallions), finely chopped
1 large egg, beaten
45 ml/3 tbsp sesame seeds, for coating
sunflower oil, for frying
salt and freshly ground black pepper

FOR THE TAHINI YOGURT DIP
30 ml/2 tbsp light tahini
200 g/7 oz/scant 1 cup plain yogurt
5 ml/1 tsp cayenne pepper, plus extra
   for sprinkling
15 ml/1 tbsp chopped fresh mint, plus extra
   for sprinkling
1 spring onion, finely sliced

Metal blade

1 Soak the chickpeas in cold water overnight. Drain and rinse, then place in a pan and cover with cold water. Bring to the boil and boil rapidly for 10 minutes, then simmer for 1½–2 hours until tender.

2 To make the dip, place the tahini, yogurt, cayenne pepper and mint in a food processor, fitted with the metal blade, and process until well blended. Transfer to a bowl, sprinkle the spring onion, extra cayenne pepper and mint on top and chill until required.

3 Combine the chickpeas with the garlic, chilli, ground spices, herbs, spring onion and seasoning, then mix in the egg. Place in the food processor and blend until the mixture forms a coarse paste. If the paste seems too soft, chill it for 30 minutes.

4 Form the paste into 12 patties with your hands, then roll in the sesame seeds to coat thoroughly.

5 Heat enough oil to cover the base of a large frying pan. Fry the falafel, in batches if necessary, for 6 minutes, turning once. Serve with the dip.

Courgette Fritters with Chilli Jam

Grate the courgettes (zucchini) for these delicious fritters in next to no time using a food processor, and use it to make the chilli jam too.

Makes 12 fritters

INGREDIENTS
450 g/1 lb courgettes (zucchini), coarsely grated in a food processor
50 g/2 oz/⅔ cup freshly grated Parmesan cheese, prepared in a food processor
2 eggs, beaten
60 ml/4 tbsp unbleached plain (all-purpose) white flour
vegetable oil, for frying
salt and freshly ground black pepper

FOR THE CHILLI JAM
75 ml/2½ fl oz/⅓ cup olive oil
4 large onions, diced in a food processor
4 garlic cloves, chopped
1–2 Thai chillies, seeded and sliced
25 g/1 oz/2 tbsp dark brown soft sugar
1 red chilli, seeded and finely sliced, to garnish

Grating disc
Metal blade

1 To make the chilli jam, heat the oil in a frying pan and add the onions and garlic. Reduce the heat to low, then cook for 20 minutes, stirring frequently, until the onions are very soft. Allow to cool.

2 Transfer the onion mixture to a food processor, fitted with the metal blade. Add the chillies and sugar and blend until smooth, then return to the saucepan. Cook for 10 minutes, stirring frequently, until the liquid evaporates and the mixture has the consistency of jam. Cool slightly.

3 Squeeze the grated courgettes in a dish towel to remove any excess water, then combine with the Parmesan, eggs, flour, salt and pepper.

4 Heat enough vegetable oil to cover the base of a large frying pan. Add 30 ml/2 tbsp of the mixture for each fritter and cook three at a time. Fry for 2–3 minutes on each side until golden.

COOK'S TIP: Stored in an airtight jar or in the refrigerator, the chilli jam will keep for up to 1 week.

5 When the first batch of fritters has cooked, remove from the pan, drain on kitchen paper and keep warm, while you cook the remaining fritters. Serve warm, accompanied by a spoonful of the chilli jam, garnished with a strip of red chilli.

Fresh Herb & Garlic Pizza

You will always want to make your own pizzas from scratch once you discover how simple it is to mix the dough, chop the topping ingredients and grate the cheese in a food processor.

Serves 4

INGREDIENTS

115 g/4 oz mixed fresh herbs
3 garlic cloves, crushed
120 ml/4 fl oz/½ cup double (heavy) cream
1 pizza base, 25–30 cm/10–12 in diameter,
　　made from 175 g/6 oz/1½ cups strong
　　white flour, 1.25 ml/¼ teaspoon salt,
　　5 ml/1 tsp easy-blend dried yeast, 120–
　　150 ml/4–5 fl oz/½–⅔ cup lukewarm
　　water, 15 ml/1 tbsp olive oil
15 ml/1 tbsp olive oil
115 g/4 oz Pecorino cheese
salt and freshly ground black pepper

Dough blade or hook
Metal blade
Grating disc

2 Place the chopped herbs, crushed garlic and cream in a bowl with salt and freshly ground black pepper to taste and mix thoroughly. Fit the grating disc to the food processor and grate the Pecorino cheese.

3 Brush the pizza base with the olive oil, then spread the herb mixture evenly over the top.

1 Preheat the oven to 220°C/425°F/Gas 7. Chop the herbs in a food processor, fitted with the metal blade.

4 Sprinkle the grated Pecorino on top of the herb mixture, and bake the pizza for 15–20 minutes until the base is crisp and golden and the topping is still moist. Cut into thin wedges and serve immediately.

Spicy Bean & Lentil Loaf

With all the chopping, grating and crumbing involved in preparing this tempting vegetarian dish, it is clear how invaluable a food processor can be.

Serves 12

INGREDIENTS

10 ml/2 tsp olive oil
1 onion, finely chopped in a
    food processor
1 garlic clove, finely chopped
2 celery sticks, finely chopped in a
    food processor
400 g/14 oz can red kidney beans
400 g/14 oz can lentils
1 egg
1 carrot, coarsely grated in a
    food processor
50 g/2 oz/½ cup finely chopped hazelnuts,
    prepared in a food processor
50 g/2 oz/½ cup finely grated mature
    Cheddar cheese, prepared in a
    food processor
50 g/2 oz/1 cup wholemeal (whole-wheat)
    breadcrumbs, made in a
    food processor
15 ml/1 tbsp tomato purée (paste)
15 ml/1 tbsp tomato ketchup
5 ml/1 tsp ground cumin, ground coriander
    and hot chilli powder
salt and freshly ground black pepper
salad, to serve

Metal blade
Grating disc

1 Preheat the oven to 180°C/350°F/ Gas 4. Lightly grease a 900 g/2 lb loaf tin. Heat the oil in a wok or pan, add the onion, garlic and celery and cook gently for 5 minutes, stirring occasionally. Remove the pan from the heat and cool slightly.

2 Drain and rinse the kidney beans and lentils. Place in a food processor, fitted with the metal blade, add the onion mixture and egg and process until smooth.

3 Transfer the mixture to a bowl, add all the remaining ingredients and mix well. Add salt and pepper to taste.

4 Spoon the mixture into the prepared tin and level the surface. Bake for about 1 hour, then remove from the tin and serve hot or cold in slices, accompanied by salad.

Coriander Ravioli with Pumpkin Filling

Make the pasta dough and the creamy filling in your food processor.

Serves 4–6

INGREDIENTS

200 g/7 oz/scant 2 cups strong unbleached white flour, plus extra for kneading
2 eggs
pinch of salt
45 ml/3 tbsp chopped fresh coriander (cilantro), plus whole sprigs and crushed seeds, to garnish

FOR THE FILLING

4 garlic cloves, unpeeled
450 g/1 lb pumpkin, peeled, seeded and diced
115 g/4 oz/½ cup ricotta
4 halves sun-dried tomatoes in olive oil, drained and finely chopped, but reserve 30 ml/2 tbsp of the oil
freshly ground black pepper

Metal blade

1 Place the flour, eggs, salt and coriander in a food processor, fitted with the metal blade. Pulse to combine.

2 Place the dough on a lightly floured board and knead well for 5 minutes, until smooth. Wrap in clear film and leave to rest in the refrigerator for 20 minutes.

3 To make the filling, preheat the oven to 200°C/400°F/Gas 6. Place the garlic cloves on a baking sheet and bake for 10 minutes until softened. Peel when cool enough to handle. Steam the pumpkin for 5–8 minutes until tender and drain well. Purée the garlic and pumpkin together with the ricotta, tomatoes and black pepper in the food processor.

4 Divide the pasta into four pieces and flatten slightly. Using a pasta machine, on its thinnest setting, roll out each piece. Leave the sheets of pasta on a clean dish towel until slightly dried. Using a 7.5 cm/3 in, crinkle-edged, round cutter, stamp out 36 rounds.

5 Top 18 rounds with a teaspoon of the filling, brush the edges with water and place another round on top. Press around the edges to seal. Bring a large pan of water to the boil, add the ravioli and cook for 3–4 minutes. Drain well and toss into the reserved tomato oil. Serve garnished with coriander sprigs and crushed seeds.

Feta Pancakes

A food processor will whip up this special batter, grate the cheese and chop the spinach for the pancake filling, to save you time and effort.

Serves 4–6

INGREDIENTS
4 eggs, beaten
40 g/1½ oz/2 tbsp butter, melted
250 ml/8 fl oz/1 cup single (light) cream
250 ml/8 fl oz/1 cup soda water
175 g/6 oz/1½ cups plain flour, sifted
pinch of salt
1 egg white, lightly beaten
oil, for frying

FOR THE FILLING
350 g/12 oz/1½ cups feta
    cheese, crumbled
50 g/2 oz/⅔ cup freshly grated Parmesan
    cheese, prepared in a food processor
40 g/1½ oz/3 tbsp butter
1 garlic clove, crushed
450 g/1 lb frozen spinach, thawed, drained
    and chopped in a food processor
fresh Parmesan cheese shavings,
    to garnish

Grating disc
Metal blade

1 Blend the eggs, butter, cream and soda water in a food processor, fitted with the metal blade. With the machine running, add the flour and salt through the feed tube to form a smooth batter. Leave to stand for 15 minutes, loosely covered with clear film.

2 Lightly grease a 13–15 cm/5–6 in non-stick frying pan and place over medium heat. When hot, pour in 45–60 ml/3–4 tbsp of the batter, tilting the pan to spread the mixture thinly.

3 Cook for about 1½–2 minutes until the underside of the pancake is pale golden brown, then turn over and cook the other side. Repeat until all the batter has been used, stacking the pancakes on a warm plate.

4 To make the filling, mix the feta, Parmesan, butter and garlic in a bowl. Squeeze as much liquid as possible from the spinach and add to the bowl.

COOK'S TIP: You can also use fresh spinach leaves for the filling if you prefer. Remove the tough stalks, rinse and steam very briefly in a covered pan, without adding any extra water. Drain well then chop in the food processor.

5 Place 30–45 ml/2–3 tbsp of the filling mixture in the centre of each pancake. Brush a little egg white around the outer edges, fold over and press down well to seal. Fry in a little oil on both sides, turning gently, until they are golden and the filling is hot. Serve immediately, garnished with Parmesan shavings.

Split Pea & Shallot Mash

This tasty alternative to mashed potatoes is easily made in a food processor.

Serves 4–6

INGREDIENTS
225 g/8 oz/1 cup yellow split peas
1 bay leaf
8 sage leaves, roughly chopped
15 ml/1 tbsp olive oil, plus extra for drizzling
  (optional)
3 shallots, finely chopped in a food processor
7.5 ml/1½ tsp cumin seeds
1 large garlic clove, chopped
50 g/2 oz/¼ cup butter, softened
salt and freshly ground black pepper
pitta bread, to serve (optional)

Metal blade

3 Meanwhile, heat the oil in a frying pan and cook the shallots, cumin seeds and garlic for 3 minutes or until the shallots soften, stirring occasionally. Add to the peas during cooking.

1 Place the split peas in a bowl and cover with cold water. Leave to soak overnight, then rinse and drain.

2 Place the peas in a pan, cover with fresh cold water and bring to the boil. Skim off any foam, then reduce the heat. Add the herbs and simmer for 30–40 minutes until tender. Add more water, if necessary.

4 Drain the split peas, reserving the cooking water. Remove the bay leaf, then place the split peas in a food processor, fitted with the metal blade. Add the butter and season well.

5 Add 105 ml/7 tbsp of the cooking water and blend to a coarse purée. Add more water if it seems dry. Adjust the seasoning and serve warm, with pitta bread and drizzled with olive oil, if liked.

Chocolate Sorbet

Use your food processor to chop both types of chocolate for this irresistible and velvety-smooth sorbet.

Serves 6

INGREDIENTS
150 g/5 oz dark (bittersweet) chocolate, chopped
115 g/4 oz plain (semisweet) chocolate, chopped
200 g/7 oz/1 cup caster (superfine) sugar
475 ml/16 fl oz/2 cups water
chocolate curls, to decorate

Metal blade

1 Put all the chocolate (except for the chocolate curls) in a food processor, fitted with the metal blade, and process for 20–30 seconds until the chocolate is very finely chopped.

2 In a pan over a medium-high heat, bring the caster sugar and water to the boil, stirring continuously until the sugar dissolves. Continue to boil the syrup for about 2 minutes, then remove from the heat.

3 With the machine running, pour the hot syrup through the feed tube on to the chocolate. Allow to run for 1–2 minutes more until the chocolate is completely melted and the mixture is smooth, scraping down the bowl once.

4 Strain the chocolate mixture into a large measuring jug or bowl. Leave to cool, then chill, stirring occasionally. Freeze the mixture in an ice-cream maker, following the manufacturer's instructions, or see Cook's Tip.

5 For best results, allow the chocolate sorbet to soften for 5–10 minutes at room temperature before serving it in scoops, decorated with the chocolate curls.

COOK'S TIP: If you do not have an ice-cream maker, freeze the sorbet until firm around the edges. Process the mixture until it is smooth, then freeze again.

Pear & Almond Cream Tart

Try this delicious recipe and you will see how truly simple it is to make brilliant pastry in a food processor.

Serves 6

INGREDIENTS

3 firm pears
juice of 1 lemon
15 ml/1 tbsp brandy or water
60 ml/4 tbsp peach preserve, strained

FOR THE PASTRY

225 g/8 oz/2 cups plain (all-purpose) flour,
  plus extra for rolling
1.5 ml/¼ tsp salt
115 g/4 oz/½ cup butter, chilled and diced
45–60 ml/3–4 tbsp iced water

FOR THE ALMOND CREAM FILLING

90 g/3½ oz/¾ cup blanched
  whole almonds
50 g/2 oz/¼ cup caster (superfine) sugar
65 g/2½ oz/5 tbsp butter
1 egg, plus 1 egg white
few drops of almond extract

Metal blade

1 To make the pastry, place the flour, salt and diced butter in the bowl of a food processor, fitted with the metal blade and process until the mixture resembles fine breadcrumbs.

2 Add the water and process briefly until the dough starts to pull away from the sides of the bowl. Gather the dough into a ball, wrap and chill.

3 Roll out the pastry thinly on a lightly floured surface and use to line a 23 cm/9 in flat tin. Chill again.

4 To make the filling, put the almonds and sugar in the food processor and pulse until finely ground; they should not be pasty. Add the butter and process until creamy, then add the egg, egg white and almond extract and mix well.

5 Place a baking sheet in the oven and preheat to 190°C/375°F/Gas 5. Peel, halve and core the pears and rub the flesh with lemon juice. Put them, cut-side down, on a large board and slice thinly crossways, keeping the slices together.

6 Pour the almond cream filling into the pastry case. Slide a palette knife under one pear half and press the top with your fingers to fan out the slices.

7 Transfer to the tart, placing the fruit on the filling like the spokes of a wheel. If you like, remove a few slices from each half before arranging and use to fill in any gaps in the centre.

8 Place the tart on the hot baking sheet and bake for 50–55 minutes or until the filling is set and well browned. Cool on a wire rack.

9 Meanwhile, heat the brandy or water and the preserve in a small saucepan, then brush over the top of the hot tart to glaze. Serve the tart at room temperature.

VARIATION: You could use blanched, unsalted pistachio nuts instead of the almonds for the filling.

Apple & Cinnamon Cake

The apples for this lovely, moist cake are grated and then combined with the butter and dates in a food processor.

Makes a 20 cm/8 in square cake

INGREDIENTS

115 g/4 oz/½ cup butter, plus extra
   for greasing
1–2 tart dessert apples, about 225 g/8 oz
200 g/7 oz/1¼ cups dried,
   stoned dates
12.5 ml/2½ tsp ground mixed (apple-pie)
   spice
2.5 ml/½ tsp salt
75 g/3 oz/½ cup raisins
2 eggs, beaten
150 g/5 oz/1¼ cups wholemeal (whole-
   wheat) flour, sifted
115 g/4 oz/generous 1 cup gram flour,
   sifted with 10 ml/2 tsp baking powder
175 ml/6 fl oz/¾ cup unsweetened
   coconut milk

Grating disc
Metal blade

1 Preheat the oven to 180°C/350°F/ Gas 4. Lightly grease a deep, 20 cm/ 8 in square baking tin and line the base with non-stick baking parchment.

COOK'S TIP: Gram flour is made from chickpeas. It is available from Asian and health food stores.

2 Peel and core the apple or apples and grate in a food processor, fitted with the grating disc. Remove from the processor and fit the metal blade.

3 Place the butter and dates in the processor, add the apple, mixed spice and salt. Process until well blended.

4 Scrape the apple and date mixture into a bowl and fold in the raisins and beaten eggs alternately with the flours, baking powder and coconut milk. Transfer to the prepared tin and smooth the surface level.

5 Bake for 30–40 minutes until dark golden and firm to the touch. A skewer inserted in the centre should come out clean. Cool the cake in the tin for 15 minutes before turning out on a wire rack to cool completely.

Little Spiced Breads

Proof that really successful bread can be produced with a food processor.

Makes 12

INGREDIENTS
120 ml/4 fl oz/½ cup warm water
5 ml/1 tsp sugar
10 ml/2 tsp active dried yeast
75 g/3 oz/6 tbsp butter, melted
15 ml/1 tbsp orange flower water or
    almond extract (optional)
400 g/14 oz/3½ cups strong white flour
75 g/3 oz/¾ cup icing (confectioners') sugar
5 ml/1 tsp salt
30 ml/2 tbsp sesame seeds
15 ml/1 tbsp fennel seeds
1 egg, beaten with 15 ml/1 tbsp water
butter and fresh dates, to serve

Dough blade or hook

1 First start the yeast. Place the warm water in a small bowl, stir in the sugar and sprinkle the yeast on top. Stir and then set aside for about 10 minutes until frothy.

2 Place the melted butter, orange flower water or almond extract, if using, and about 175 ml/6 fl oz/¾ cup warm water in a separate bowl and stir to mix. Stir the flour, icing sugar, salt, sesame seeds and fennel seeds together in the bowl of a food processor, fitted with the dough blade or hook.

3 Add the yeast and half of the butter and water mixture to the flour and process so that they slowly combine. Continue processing, adding the remaining butter and water to make a smooth, glossy dough. (You may need to add extra flour or warm water.)

4 Continue for 1–2 minutes, then transfer to a floured surface and knead by hand for a few minutes until the dough is smooth and elastic.

5 Place in a clean, lightly oiled bowl, cover with clear film and leave in a warm place for 1–1½ hours until doubled in size. Knead again for a few minutes, break into 12 small balls and flatten slightly with oiled hands. Place on a greased baking sheet, cover with oiled clear film and let rise for 1 hour.

6 Preheat the oven to 190°C/375°F/ Gas 5. Brush the breads with egg and then bake in the oven for 12–15 minutes or until golden. Serve warm or cold with butter and fresh dates.

Saffron Focaccia

Mix the dough for this dazzling yellow, distinctively flavoured classic Italian bread in your food processor.

Makes 1 loaf

INGREDIENTS
pinch of saffron threads
150 ml/¼ pint/⅔ cup boiling water
225 g/8 oz/2 cups strong plain (all-purpose)
    white flour, plus extra for kneading
2.5 ml/½ tsp salt
5 ml/1 tsp easy-blend dried (rapid-rise) yeast
15 ml/1 tbsp olive oil, plus extra for oiling

FOR THE TOPPING
2 garlic cloves, sliced
1 red onion, cut into thin wedges
fresh rosemary sprigs
12 pitted black olives, coarsely chopped in
    a food processor
15 ml/1 tbsp olive oil

Metal blade
Dough blade or hook

1 Place the saffron in a heatproof container and pour on the boiling water. Leave to stand and infuse until lukewarm.

2 Place the flour, salt, easy-blend dried yeast and olive oil in a food processor, fitted with the dough blade or hook. Turn the machine on and gradually add the saffron and its soaking liquid through the feed tube. Process until the dough forms into a ball.

3 Turn on to a floured surface and knead for 10–15 minutes. Place in a lightly oiled bowl, cover with oiled clear film and leave in a warm place to rise for 30–40 minutes until the dough has doubled in size.

4 Knock back the risen dough on a floured surface and roll out into an oval shape, 1 cm/½ in thick. Place on a lightly oiled baking sheet, and leave to rise for 20–30 minutes.

5 Preheat the oven to 200°C/400°F/ Gas 6. Use your fingers to press small indentations all over the upper surface of the focaccia, but do not go through the base.

6 Cover the bread with the topping ingredients, brushing lightly with olive oil, and bake for 25 minutes or until the loaf sounds hollow when tapped on the bottom. Leave to cool on a wire rack, before serving.

Index

This edition is published by Lorenz Books,
an imprint of Anness Publishing Ltd,
Blaby Road, Wigston, Leicestershire LE18 4SE; info@anness.com
www.lorenzbooks.com; www.annesspublishing.com

If you like the images in this book and would like to investigate using them for publishing, promotions or advertising, please visit our website www.practicalpictures.com for more information.

A CIP catalogue record for this book is available from the British Library.

Publisher: Joanna Lorenz
Editor: Valerie Ferguson & Helen Sudell
Series Designer: Bobbie Colgate Stone
Designer: Andrew Heath
Production Controller: Wendy Lawson

Photography: William Adams-Lingwood, Karl Adamson, James Duncan, Ian Garlick, Michelle Garrett, Amanda Heywood, Janine Hosegood, David Jordan, Patrick McLeavey, Thomas Odulate.

Recipes contributed by: Catherine Atkinson, Michelle Berriedale-Johnson, Angela Boggiano, Carla Capalbo, Carole Clements, Trish Davies, Sarah Edmonds, Christine France, Silvano Franco, Shirley Gill, Nicola Graimes, Rebekah Hassan, Christine Ingram, Judy Jackson, Lesley Mackley, Norma MacMillan, Sallie Morris, Annie Nichols, Anne Sheasby, Liz Trigg, Steven Wheeler, Elizabeth Wolf-Cohen, Jeni Wright.

COOK'S NOTES

Bracketed terms are intended for American readers.

For all recipes, quantities are given in both metric and imperial measures and, where appropriate, in standard cups and spoons. Follow one set of measures, but not a mixture, because they are not interchangeable.

Standard spoon and cup measures are level. 1 tsp = 5ml, 1 tbsp = 15ml, 1 cup = 250ml/8fl oz. Australian standard tablespoons are 20ml. Australian readers should use 3 tsp in place of 1 tbsp for measuring small quantities.

American pints are 16fl oz/2 cups. American readers should use 20fl oz/2.5 cups in place of 1 pint when measuring liquids.

Electric oven temperatures in this book are for conventional ovens. When using a fan oven, the temperature will probably need to be reduced by about 10–20°C/20–40°F. Since ovens vary, you should check with your manufacturer's instruction book for guidance.

Medium (US large) eggs are used unless otherwise stated.

PUBLISHER'S NOTE: